Pascale Leconte

MANTRAS coloring BOOK

Illustrations : cdd20 (pixabay.com)

© 2020 Pascale Leconte.
Éditeur : BoD-Books on Demand
12-14 rond-point des Champs-Élysées, 75008 Paris
Impression : Books on Demand, Norderstedt, Allemagne
Dépôt légal : June 2020.
ISBN : 9782322235049

I DON'T HAVE ANY EXPECTATIONS

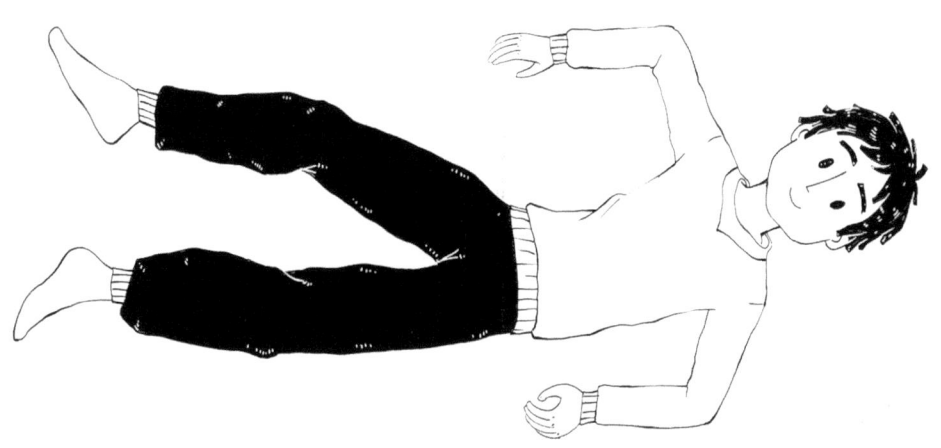

EVERYTHING IS ALREADY THERE

GOOD AND EVIL ARE TWO SIDES OF THE SAME COIN. THIS COIN IS ME. THIS COIN IS EVERYTHING. GOOD AND EVIL ARE TWO SIDES OF THE SAME COIN. THIS COIN IS ME. THIS COIN IS EVERYTHING.

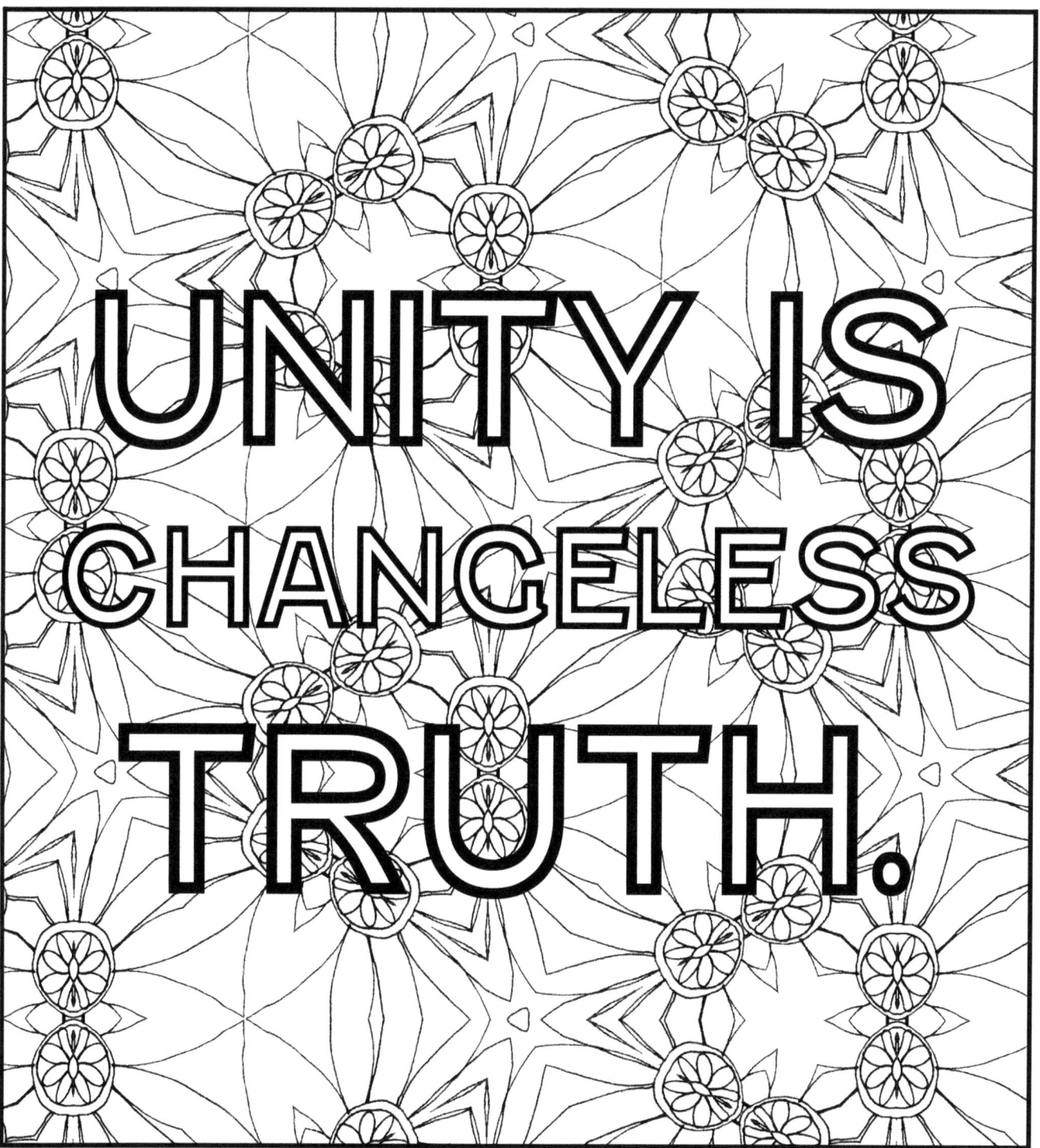

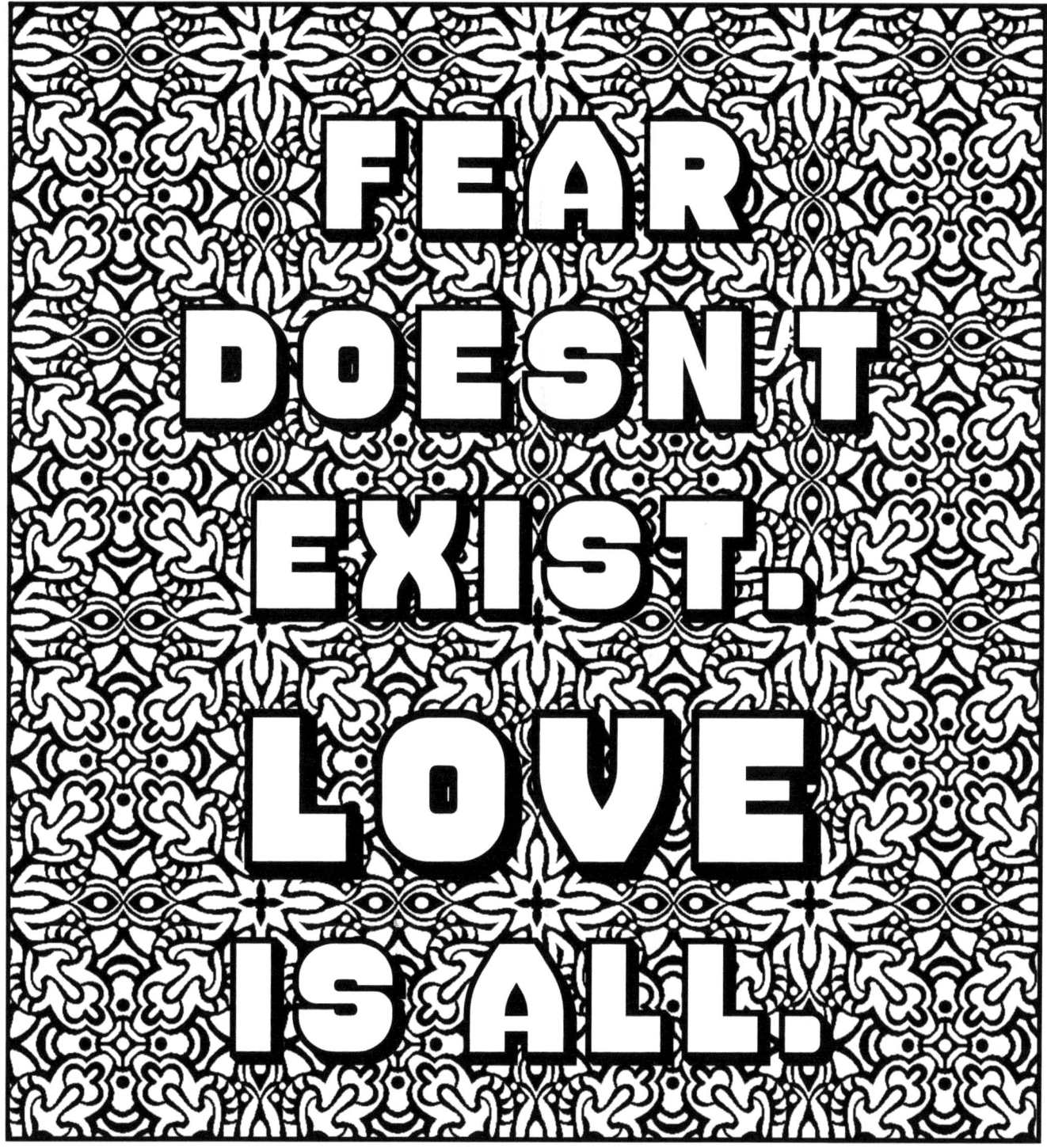

I AM PURE LOVE.
I AM PURE LOVE.
I AM PURE LOVE.
I AM PURE LOVE.
I AM PURE LOVE.
I AM PURE LOVE.
I AM PURE LOVE.
I AM PURE LOVE.

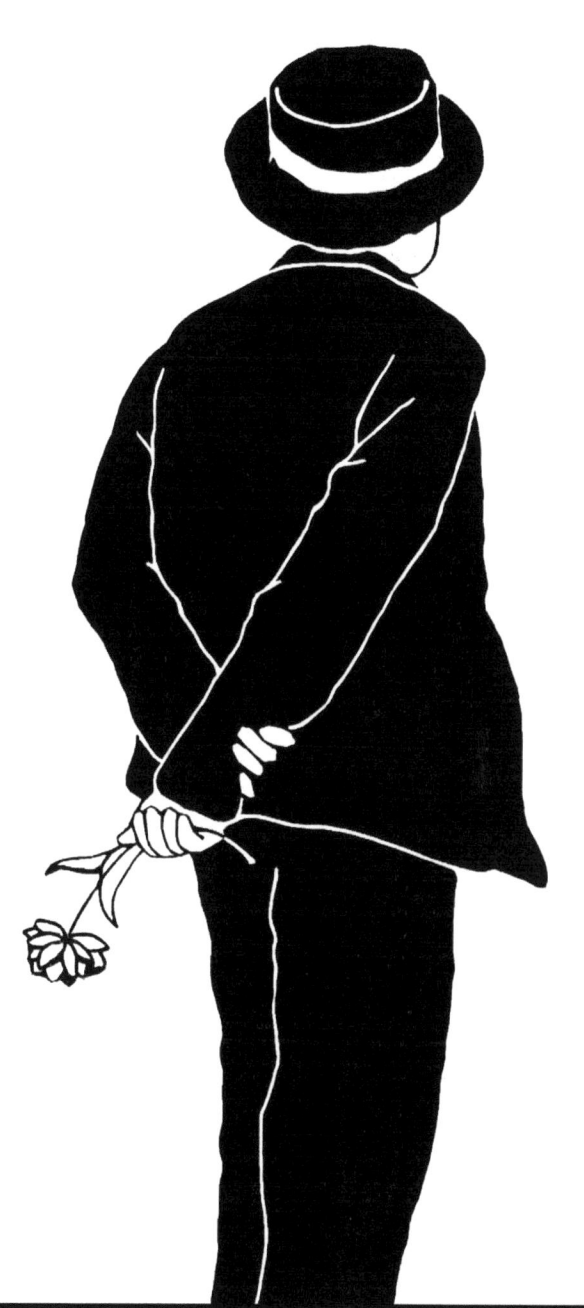

Only the Present counts. Only this Instant counts. Only the Present counts. Only this Instant counts.

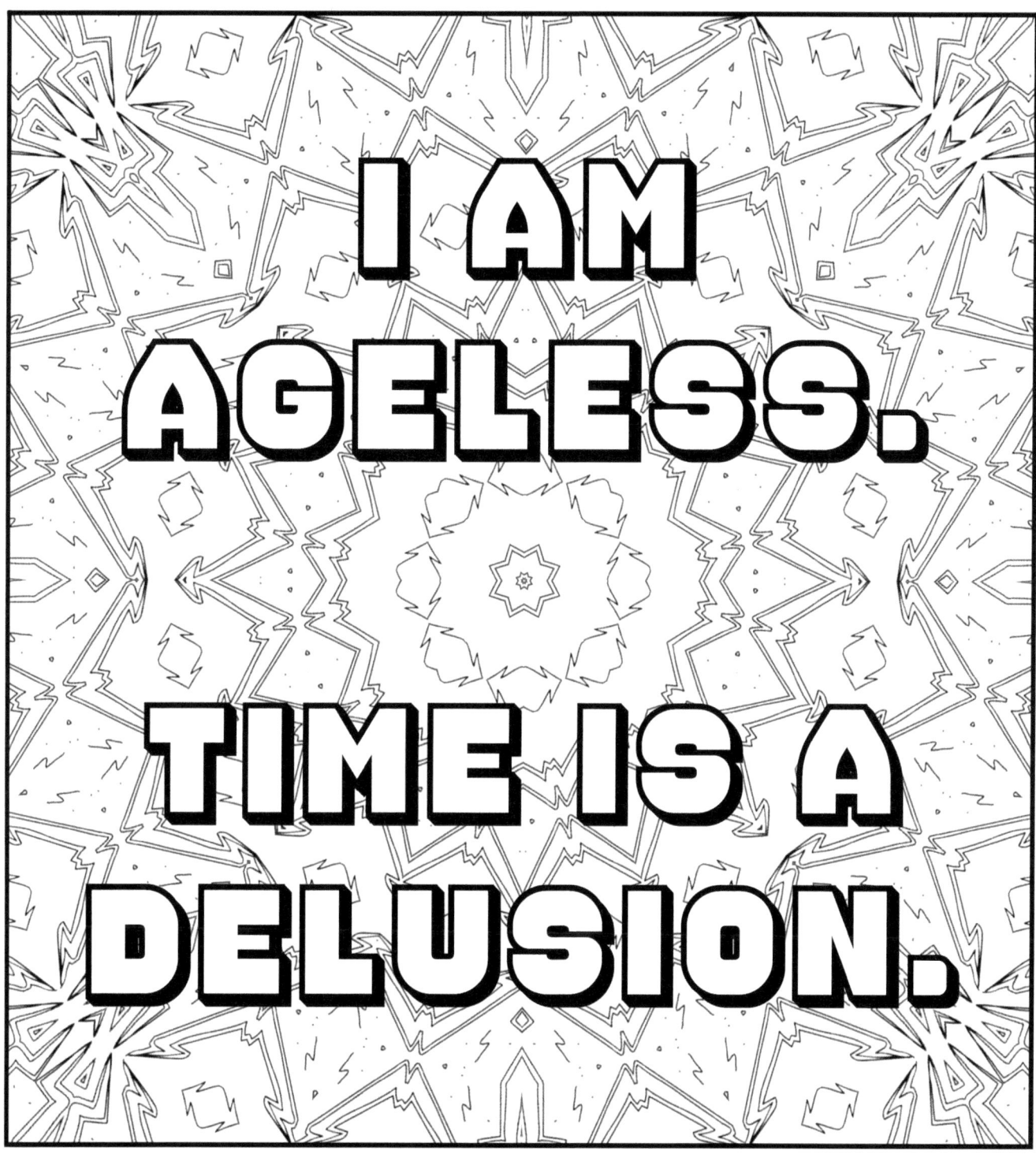

Whether I love him or hate him, I am he. He is me.

UNCONDITIONAL LOVE
UNCONDITIONAL LOVE
UNCONDITIONAL LOVE
UNCONDITIONAL LOVE
UNCONDITIONAL LOVE
UNCONDITIONAL LOVE
UNCONDITIONAL LOVE
UNCONDITIONAL LOVE
UNCONDITIONAL LOVE

I RESPECT MYSELF. I RESPECT MY BODY. I RESPECT MY LIMITS. I RESPECT MY DECISIONS.

I observe the emotions running through me.
I am not those emotions.
They just pass through me.

I AM
SOVEREIGN
OVER MY
OWN LIFE.
I LET GO OF
THE LIVES
OF OTHERS.

I LISTEN TO MY JOY. IT'S MY INNER COMPASS.

IN PReSeNCe

IN PReSeNCe

IN PReSeNCe

IN PReSeNCe

IN PReSeNCe

Other publications by the same author:

From Homo Sapiens to Homo Deus:
How to complete Man's evolution?
— BOD Editions

Jack the Ripper is not a man
— Amazon Editions

The little book of Mantras to be whispered
— BOD Editions